Praise for *Night breaks apart, like pomegranate seeds in my palm*

'Aakriti Kuntal's is a highly charged sensory world. The poems are aggregations of explosive haikus, each part like a sharp stepping stone to the next. There is certainly passion here, and a process of reconciliation with energies barely in control. The images are seen in flashes of light. "I spill white like the flashing night / and I never burn," she writes. But the poems do burn.' —George Szirtes

'There are very few people who can see "the sharp fang of light", "an insect strapped to the day's chest", "naked boredom", or "death as a compound". Aakriti Kuntal's poems surprise at every turn. She is one of my favourite Indian poets.'—Sumana Roy

'These poems are meditations on life within death—death within life. One stands in the eye of a hurricane—generative forces of creation and destruction all around. In bushwhacking through the sensations that arise from reading these poems, one comes upon a trembling animal—grieving for it—loving it—consoling it. "I know I'm a red song / that you once took in / your arms, mother . . . "'—Gary Lemons

Aakriti Kuntal is a poet, writer and multidisciplinary artist. She spends most of her time writing and reading, seeking refuge in nature. At other times, she explores photography, asemic writing, visual art and short experimental films. Her work has appeared in *The Night Heron Barks*, *Rasputin: A Poetry Thread*, *IceFloe Press*, *Cha: An Asian Literary Journal*, and *Poetry at Sangam*, among others. She is the author of the chapbook *God, am I your eyelid?* (Sigilist Press, USA). Her accolades include the Reuel International Prize (2017); she was shortlisted for the RL Poetry Award (2018) and nominated for Best of the Net.

AAKRITI KUNTAL

Night breaks apart, like pomegranate seeds in my palm

Poems

LONDON NEW YORK CALCUTTA

THE INDIA LIST

Seagull Books, 2025

First published by Seagull Books, 2025

ISBN 978 1 80309 575 2

British Library Cataloguing-in-Publication Data
A catalogue record for this book is available from the British Library

Typeset by Seagull Books, Calcutta, India

CONTENTS

Bulb

Scab

Flagella

Cytoplasm

Bulb

BLINK

What is this vow hibernating on the crest of lip?
Drifting from sleep to awareness to sleep again;
A red hibiscus in the cardiogram of being,
A vacillating desire to breathe immensely

EVENING

Evening,
a marble plateau,
sliced breath of the day

Red pomegranate seeds splutter,
turning the mouth's estranged sky
into a velvet sienna

Stillness—
lack of movement
or lack of thought?

An elongation of emotion
a requiem for the living

The air, it seems,
is suffused with a flat, ochre light,
static around the bark of all trees

A consolation,
a lullaby,
a long, long pause
everything in the goddamn world
bending down
to stare at its very own miracle

Twilight's veil flutters,
an insect strapped to the day's chest

She moves,

Slowly,
Carefully—
there are no mistakes made here
the day falls in precise moments,
just as it began

A cold shudder

A celestial beast
salivates over life's porous face

And the horizon grins

Evening,
the sly tongue of light

PRESENCE

Evening engulfs my warm waist
and brightens it,
I am a clay goddess

There is a hesitation in all skin,
its aimless existence

I open my mouth
and do not feel any breath,
only a quiet climate,
a sting

A flower droops into my vision
It is desperate to be observed,
to be known

Is acknowledgement an affirmation of life?

Presence

I shut my eyes
and the sky is blueberries,
a child's frock
swivelling above earth

A flower
continues to be
above my continually diffusing chin,

An incense stick

Its elongated time
now rustling within my submerged flesh

Presence
is the dialogue
between two desperate beings

WHIRR

A bumblebee
whirrs,
its triangular wings in the mouth of air

Slipping through the past, present—
                                                            time

Drifting   across   the   condensed pores

Here,
a light, a breeze as bright
and sharp—
      as a fang

The bones tuned to the orchestra
grimly watch the shedding dust,

The quarters of lost sunrays
the bumblebee moves—

No purpose,
only desire—desire both sweet and heavy

Desire, invisible yet palpable,
bursting similarly at the seams of my fingers

The bumblebee,
bright in the eye,
a spark   sh ift ing   in space

Above the abode of fuchsia flowers,
their homely heads submerged
in a permanent vacation from the earth;
surrendered to the foaming winds in the last of days

The bumblebee,
  bright   sharp
snipping the air, cutting it into bosoms of longing

Until one catches the other
and the other leaves another

And the body,
both seamless and restless
is cut and unified in a long, nameless song

CHOIR

Tusks of light
scratch
a starch blue sky

In the restaurant, people move,
move continuously; their mouths imitating
the same plural motions of their bodies

A curious fragility
in this obstinate need

A child's balloon skirt
flies past my eye,
ricocheting—into the sigh of all living things

Not all motion is the same

This one
is how laughter would seem
if sketched along the Cartesian coordinates,
over time's gentle rim

The others move to and fro,
catching nothing but air

Like limbs
they find purpose
in the mechanical spheres,
a naked boredom in the stutter

Outside the restaurant,
the magnesian green shrubs
display a startling lack of movement

They seem to have been bitten
by a tale of silence—

Thick, pink air hovering,
velvet saliva over meditating skin

I stare at them for a while,
pondering . . .

If I look long enough,
would I too dissolve in their vastness of green?

IVORY SPELL

Mauve teeth
          shre dd ed threads of winter
slanted, sprouting heads
wet algae
on the blushing rim of silver wells

A numb violet
slides
along your banshee cerebrum,

Visits the spurting neck,
teal-pastel eucalyptus and moaning ice
chalk dispersion and water veneer

Your face
carries the wreckage of the Indian Ocean,
the rush of squeezed blue shores

Your face
carries ignominy and tender mischief,
sipping from the ancient dregs of deforestation

You sprinkle
icicles in the vulva

Growing tentacles
of uncertainty

Engulf the creek,

the nymph stretches of grass,
the faint sheet of life

Cold,
cold,
merciless

LILITH

Lilith,
sepulchre of stunted air

A thin laugh—
the drooping Venus-tongues
ecstatic in the wedges of space

My garden blistered with their warm breath,
their constant heaving

Their inaudible, glaring presence
thousands of purple baby-fists

Hanging, just
        hanging

The most precious of sights
yet appalling,
very appalling

Lilith,
your large, viscous being
above these pockets of breasts

You stand
with your tongue deep in my mouth,
a fine straw of divine ache

You stand—still,
deviously devoid of all language,

You stand,
seeking neither forgiveness
nor awaiting any,

You stand outside,
outside breath, sense, being,

You stand,
outside of all human judgement—
plain vicious,

the glorious face of luscious lunacy

VINES

The black fruits are ripe—
perched in a delicate silence

Clasped fists
    the dark centre slowly stirs
sun's breathless core

The diamond grape,
rich as a dream
a full life in the giant's mouth,
wholesome and sumptuous

Outside the window,
a dream is running barefoot
naked among the vines
oiling all with its velveteen slime

Outside the window,
an eye is lost
in the eternal static of the white night

Outside the window,
neither father nor mother
neither love nor death

Outside the window,
an invisible fire

The great burden of murmurs,
the faithless bark of heads

Outside the window,
most blatant ecstasy,
a mulberry lake of frigid quiet

Outside the window,
breath, breath
nothing but sheets of wispy breath,
as cold
as eternal
as the stone's riverine eye

SPURT

Each spring,
I lay open
a seed halved,
hammer to the bone

I spread
blades of pink flesh,
thistles slicing proximity into anticipation

I squirm—
gather around my being

Mud beneath the grass
to cough up weary dreams

VITAL LANGUAGES

A momentary lapse in the sky's mouth,
colours stream

The vital language of sun
scratches the feverish body of a flower

Body parts like petals
soak and combust
grow into ten thousand moments,
all at once

Each pore—a tentacle
dangling along the startled air

The arm—a curve
covers the view, the world

Shut off,
the body travels into the sky

And the vital language of sun
meets the vital language of thirst

A NAMELESS TREACHERY BY THE WINDOWSILL

A wallow of whale-blue light
a perennial day

Perspires
along the neat triangle
of table peace

Something about
the setting is dishonest

I cannot seem to discern

The lamp skull
withdraws into a sly,
whiskered smile

While the window
seems to be burning
with nothing

There are hot,
hot fumes
and the cheeks
sink into a queasy suspension

Autumn drifting past them,
barely saying a word

I smell
matchsticks cut through the air,

the sweet stench of betrayal
hissing in air pockets

Meanwhile,
birds crisscross
an even blue sky

And the leaves are sweet,
delectable in their embroidered green

Yet the fingers,
the fingers run,
run as buttermilk across black dreams

And I cannot seem
to gulp the brevity

that is creation
that a single window can witness
such polarized scenes

MY HEART AT SUNRISE

Light circulates behind the window,
seamstress of orange ferns

I take my widowed palms
into a large spin
and set them on fire,
auburn against the day's soft sun

Cease and count—
the sacred lungs of fire
as they awaken the sky today
once more,
one last time

Cease and count
the lifting colours of dead bees
as they roam—
strung across a sleepless blue continent

Cease and demarcate—
the furious longevity,
the rugged intervals
that lick my lonely breaths
and throttle the stunned air

Distort
a quiet blue sky
into this dreamless raging voice

as only ugly passions like ours do;
then let it beat—
outside of all creation

My falling heart at sunrise

LOTUS

Upwards,
these lips—boat-like,
inundating rivers
within their pondering girth

Upwards,
this skin—cellophane treasures
collecting colour
from the sky's subservience

Upwards,
hand, mouth, body
organs shattering
in coalescent proximity

I raise my head
to an uneven sun,
watch its cadenced portions

Clouds ablaze against
the hum of detonation

I raise my body,
my skin,
my entire being,
my cheeks frosting
like cream

The irregular elongation
of life's symptoms,
a fat ellipse around
my belly

I raise my departed teeth,
my chiselled naivety

I buzz and blink,
my face a periwinkle pink,
the forgotten trick
of forgetfulness
clawing at my lip

I draw the navel to my mouth
and perch like a lotus,
swirl amid tectonic suns

I raise
my body,
my skin,
my entire being
I spill white like the flashing night
and I never burn

Scab

AN EVENT IN THE NEIGHBOURHOOD

I adopt
a movement
like air

Wading along the mind's eye
through the obvious,
the oblivious,

The steam of all perspiring things

The moon
stares at nothing—
cold eye of the sky,
the quality of a stone
in its eternal passiveness

Someone died
in the house behind the house

There are no signs here in my garden
only the ellipse of faint knowledge

I sit cross-legged in my chair,
breeze flowing, sparks between
scissor-feet
I perch,
a bamboo spiral,
nearly immortal
in the half-stasis of heaving air

I perch,
dissolving
inconspicuously into a bleak
          nothingness

Pale, oblong rain
strumming against flaps of salmon skin

                              Someone died
in the house behind the house

And suddenly,
death too seems
as uneventful and minuscule as life

THROUGH TIME AND BODY

Does the body cremate itself in time
or is it time
that is cremated in the body?

Restless hours hang by the doorknob,
quietly observing the spin of skin
transparent skeletons become of days—

Spewing black tar over trails

The shadow walks like a detached face,
purest in the night
atom meeting atom, colour inhaling colour

Softly, swallowing all sounds,
it finds a way into the larynx,
fingers in the oesophagus collecting laments of the voice

It draws a map beneath the eye—
the map of a noise
squirming syllables, rattlesnakes
invasion of air, invasion of dust

All light is a refugee in the body
flitting scales, itches, flashes and glitter
all light is a purple throb

Beneath,
night slithers,
her ionized hair curtailing all movement of the skies

STRATOSPHERIC SEDUCTION

Streams of air
constructed like rivers above the stomach

Fluids and sediments
lisping along the navel

Thighs submerged in atmospheric slush

I take my bereft fingers
and uproot the throbbing lip
of swollen sienna

Lip crests above lip

foreground
                    underground
                         softness, crusts, crumbs
                             taut, red
tension, adhesives
      elasticity
                  dirt, dust, dust, dirt
                              particles
                         coalescence agony
congruence

orgasm

Within the circumference of the navel,
a forest is lit
tubes and tunnels of temperature unwind

chop-chop

The lumberjack walks in arrogance;
life likes to take without permission
what it gave without permission

I inhale the slippery face of night,
my nostrils
cold as mountain ranges

Life's favourite romance is with death

ANATOMY OF DEATH—IN TIME

Death is a compound,
a process, a cold verb

Every day the trees shudder
they have stood too long,
they know

That death is a compound,
not a finality or an accident
but dilution,

A repetition
until absorbed, until accepted

Until then
death is a long, gluey chewing gum
and my mouth is under vascular surgery

Look at the clouds murder themselves,
then spread prostrate on whale-grey roads

Here it is that I stand—
an observer, a victim,
a corpse, a child, a tree, a tree, a shrub
and death,

Death is the perennial gown

ABDUCTION

White salt out there,
your whitewashed twigs scowl—
motions unfamiliar

The night is growing thick;
the finger is aflame, a matchstick

It has sworn to shimmer;
the teeth abandon the jaw
and float into the sea,

A jawbone into the sea's eternity
a poet stood before the ocean

And never returned,
return he did not

And in my cupped eyelid,
a quarter of the moon, the man's weakening
steps, a half knee dipped in water green,

Arms swinging like ropes,
their jolly—an unfathomable absurdity

Every day the sea washes
his stench from shells and crab skins

Every day the sea washes the sand's antenna feet

A poet walked into the sea
and never returned

Flagella

THE SERPENT

I.

Thrust
water   springing
slush
white, white eye   half-moon eye
            a burning galaxy

And the red dimness
hovering in the shadow of the cup

A premonition

A final leap—
      and then blood

The serpent rises as mud from the earth's lap

Abandoned by all,
it has not the face for love

It crawls the slippery soil,
the sewn valleys—dense, secret holes in amber

The serpent—
hisses alone under the clear blue sky

Hissing, hissing, hissing
an enormous restlessness,
an eternal restlessness biting its tongue

II.

The serpent became
when the earth fell
and the first star collapsed

Brown, molten, striped
the earth's mad forehead—
tears, streams, violent spurts

The serpent became
when the earth fell;
rising as the mud's only wail,
filled with murder and rage

It rotates its only head
in eternal restlessness,
rising, hissing, rising

Traversing nights and days
with its limbs stripped,

Its unusual body of slime
traversing the very boundaries of the earth

The serpent rises in murderous thirst—

An orphaned star

AN ORDINARY STONE

I bring a stone home;
it is nothing extraordinary

It is plain
if plain were to be defined—
it is that,
just one more diagram of gravity's will
mass acknowledging mass

It is not the skinned fervour of dusk
or a jigsaw puzzle of napkin dreams;
it possesses no brightness
nor is it smooth like the tongue's drool

It is just an ordinary stone,
only an ordinary blankness
which has seen the earth birth and ovulate

In its cold shell,
the history of oceans and streams

An eye that speaks only to the
rugged wind,
the wind its only lover,
bringing quiet stretch marks

It is an ordinary stone,
an ordinary stone it is—
dull   lifeless   cold black eye
fallen wet submerged

You touch it
and you glimpse the other side of eternity,
a black mask—
listening to everything,
part of nothing

SEA

The sea sleeps in its eternal blackness.
I throw a stone
and the sea eats it.

I throw an arm,
a body, a smile, a tear, some cough
and the sea eats it.

The sea stretches from the horizon
to the cold forehead,
covering everything in its feverish grey light.

I throw a clot of blood
and the sea—like a snake,
coils into a watery dream.

Shivers as the serpent
with its scales falling off,
cotton skies.

I throw a lie
and the sea catches it;
giggles and throws it right back at me.

The waves splash in my face,
their sounds hiccup endlessly in my ears.

I throw myself to the sea
and the sea inhales me.

Sea,
giant god of everything.

NAME

A name
is the most unusual predicament,
barely resembling the thing itself

It makes it come alive.
a name,
however carelessly strewn, however inept,

However uncharacteristic
bears the totem of affection.
a person or a thing

Becomes whole in a name;
without names
we are anonymous wanderers—

Flits in the window,
all too alike, all too different,
yet none distinct from the other.

It is an intersection of consonants,
vowels interspersed, the countenance of sounds,
the guttural efficacy of the body

To reach out to something larger than itself.
a name
is an arrow in space,

A pointer—not space itself

but a reference
like a binary value

Indicating the energy
one occupies
in the memory of time.

A name
is a strand, a fine strand,
a red ribbon that winds unto itself

And yet exists in the sinusoidal saliva of all being.
a name bestows identity;
man is bound to his name

Like a thread to a finger,
the blood so purple—so thick,
it becomes the very rush of life

And yet a name
is the most ridiculous title one could ever wear,
so meticulously woven

But so bereft of purpose and meaning.
none are born with a name;
nothing has a name outside human cognizance

Yet names are assigned—
they are our most subtle way
of ascribing value to something,

Our most elemental gift
to life
and its constituents.

THE TRAJECTORY OF A POEM

A poem isn't born
when it is written
you cannot—determine its time of birth

A poem revels in this uncertainty
it is a subatomic particle
it is a lover

It elopes   into the wide absence;
perhaps,   where it has always been,
the loose   hhhhuummm   of   time   and   space

You wish to mark its location,
build a trajectory for your comprehension
but it is clever,
so much cleverer than you

It knows the Heisenberg Uncertainty Principle
and it wishes
to continually evade

You know this poem
you have carried it—
a throb,
    a knot,
        a roOOAAar,
            a shriekkkk,
an orgasm

You sense it has been in you for a while now
it has absorbed your blood,
it carries your piquant aroma

A poem is an inverted tree. It occurred
simultaneously on separate days, in separate places—

The swollen shadow of your mother's voice
a red spot on your face
the innocent tale of bees
in childhood's garden
the bewildered hibiscus
the uprooted sun
and his feverish earth
the missing kiss
the scented lover

A poem is a dance,
something stirring in your mouth
a poem meditates into existence

It wades
through perceptions and inflections,
across silences and valleys

A poem
is a mountain on paper
and you—its living shadow

DEAR ‘ ’

You i
You with a cr()ss face
o

A mesh
A diagram An uNe*v*En joy

A notion
A necessity
An unconfirmed truth

A ——puncture—— in the pink, flammable sky

You without a name,
without a b
o
d
y

You—with a pair of blue eyes
continuously **cauterizing** the breadth of days

You,
this poem sits upon your n
o
s
e

This poem is the aftermath of a moth,

a moth   with   s-o-l-d-e-r-e-d   wing*S*   and   h*ea*vi*n*g   skin.

This poem is empty,
so empty.

Its stomach roars   soaked cotton
a valley of residues   a **Clo**t
a white shell sea with boat lips
~~~~~~~~~~~~~~~~~~~~~~~~

This poem is the   sha*d*<u>ow</u>   of life
it is   l o *n*   *g*   and   heavy   and it cares
about neither contour nor shape;

It only possesses a fever,
a froth of blue saliva on its tumbling tongue

This poem is the bLiNkInG song of your
des
cen
ding
iris

It wishes to settle like dust abOve it
it yearns to taste the sentence of your eye,
its   stre t   ch   i   ng   ar**ch**es,
its amorphous horizons

This poem keeps writing and rewriting itself
this poem is a verb   —>strangled<—   between us

This poem is a stone in a   dreaming   mouth,
too heavy to be pronounced
~~~~~~~~~~~~~~~~~~~~~~~~

An entirety waiting to be foLDed into oblivion
this poem aches this poem seeks
this poem almost wants,
wants you

You?

Are you?

Who are you?

Are you the endless, bleached sigh of the skies
the miR|Ror of the cloud that is breath,
the tr*emo*r that one cannot name,
the flat silence between nights?

You,

this poem's faraway lover,
its carbon home,

This poem
seeks
you

CITY DRIVE

You say
the cars seem to float
among invisible gray whales,
a sheet of slippery sea beneath our peddling feet

The body of the city
is lit,
red balls of yarns in the queen's closet,
as if beckoning closure, awaiting a larger moment

The body of the city,
unfettered beneath the moon,
a pan of milk in an untidy sky

Your skin,
gathered similarly into a gasp
beneath that one dimple,
the one that sits—a monk in sycamore trees

Your body—
close, knotted,
a forest
entering and leaving me
in places uncountable
a touch that doesn't fit into any language
a touch—both earth and fire

You say the cars float above an invisible sea,
your frame

passionate in its composition—
reaffirming my sentence by its very presence

You say the cars float above an invisible sea

Your breath—
an inexhaustible joy

Your body—
an entire city I seek

Our eyes—
like whales in an invisible sea

TENDER CONSONANTS

Your name—a peach in the mouth,
a shiny orange bundle of light
that bounces between the teeth.

In your name—the effortlessness
of vowels, the consonance of
sounds. Your name—

The epigraph of our tongues, their
rolling sweetness that sticks
like gum and refuses to let go.

Your name—the bearer of kisses,
a seashell where our echoing lives
are born again. Your name is where

I empty my cardigans and wool,
where my heart's dreary winter
can rest. Your name is the crest

On which my lonely days tilt
into litters of joy. Your name—
a slit in the lip, its juice spurting

From both body and spirit.

After Marina Tsvetaeva's 'Poems for Blok'

Synapse

I. The-Lung-Is-A-Black-Balloon

SOMNIUM

Something fluid in the collarbone,
something
that slithers, that watches
with a keen button eye

A lonely diamond in a tilted mouth—
a sparkle
the bewildered night
rests
like a jewel between sacks of clotted skies

I surmise
I am asleep
and the shadow of life is perched—
on my chest

Arched
against the limestone ceiling
strumming   my empty cotton breast
mocking   its plain, life-like desires

Water boils,
inundates the petticoat

I'm afloat

Something tells me

that my ear is being chewed
and that my body
is a long, long never-ending lie

Something moves
around my saline neck, coiling,
something—unspeakable and bright
behind every corner of the eye

Something vivid,
warm,
and blood-like

Almost like life,
almost like death
but something between the two—
the godless face of a cry

CONCUSSION

Corpuscles
stream down, accumulate
around the basin of feet

Toes—
islands on a sheet of molecules,
molecules of curdled air,
half skin, half breath

The umbilical song bleeds from the curtain

Leaving the window
perspiring
against the dewy daylight—jaggery strokes

An aftermath
of being,
of its calamitous stench,
a pool of piss on fire . . .

An aftermath,
birth
and a lingering patch of life;

A warm, pulsating concussion
on time's white, gleaming forehead

What is this   that seems to leak
from the hands

the fingers   the oak-white nails,
these filaments of warm air
ballooning
beneath the nostril?

What is this
nauseating gulf of life
that drains
before it fills—swallows cherry-shaped infant lives?

Their edematose feet
now hung
inside the lung of a flaccid red sky

A SLIT IN TIME

A deep, violet flutter
a biting flower
a slit across the forehead of time

Plaque-ridden teeth gnawing,
a ball of yarn—coming loose
in the mouth

The warm, yellow tongue
stuck
in a wrap of epileptic pauses

The lead trees still hold the sky hostage

Scraping for answers,
flailing
their gathered fist-bowls

Palpitating
lacewings

                                        An entire life—
loose in opaque rivers and paranoid leeks,
in green-eyed lobes and white blood hyphens

An entire life—
    toe to knuckle,
    jaw to disc,
    blade to clavicle,

bone beside bone beside bone

Forever levitating
inside rings
of condensed lavender time

BIPOLAR

Something between death
and the idea of death—

A blackberry bludgeoned
into a plush dream,
creeks of blood salivating on the windowpane

The windowpane is heavy
everything seems to pass through it

A cyan rush—a scream,
foam, sky, scissors, and needles,
people, so many
flat-faced and bean-eyed people

Only the numbness perpetuates—
rows and rows of trapped light,
a wedge in the centre that pierces from both ends

Only,
the large, enormous cough of being,
droplets of life in a whitewashed sky

And all of life—
        hands   flailing flesh
pink nuclei   scales of pigeon-grey necks

All of life's brimming waves
squeezed into a hazy vomit,
a funnel of non-being

The windowpane
incandescent as a chiselled moon
simmers in its invisible restlessness

Rendered essentially colourless—
bone to tendon
space to density
fluid to air

The windowpane,
a box of volatile wings,
floats between cement cubes—
perforated,
sculpted,
God's eternal face carved into a translucent sleep

SPECKS

Somewhere,
a particle percolates
a shining sliver of blood courses up

          Into the petticoat,
the mass of thick thighs,
the sectors of sliced air

A corpse's inverted smile
around the navel's washed light

I imagine now—
maybe, I'm approaching backwards
that perhaps . . .
perhaps,
the grey waters of the eye are soft purrs,

Pools of cyan bloodstreams,
lost blood
          blood, blood, blood
nothing is as pure,
as eternally restless,
as determined
and without purpose
as these bouts of blood
behind my steel-grey eye

In my mouth,
the flaccid stem of a flower

In my mouth,
the formless face of skies,
utterances clogging their fluorescent frocks

The sky of life,
a diffused dot,
clutching its legs,
holding a dream between its tiny toes

And the night,
the night,
unsteady as a shudder,
enclosing every breath, every light

Maybe, it is backwards,
death to death,
death to life

Maybe, it is backwards,
and my chest isn't brown
but blue, very blue

Something dead aims to knock
at the evening's flitting air—
an almost delightful sheen
across these dilapidated teeth

SORORITY

Years hum—
dense churning of air beside the ear

A loose, round, elongated beat
a rhythm?
perhaps, a hiccup, a vomit, a wail—cluttered

The trees match this syncopation of my tongue—
of my tongue
against this tide of being,
shuffling between intimate spaces of darkness

Perhaps, they too are sick?
particles of dirt
evaporate from their skewed algae arms
only to settle again into a pattern of disgrace

An utter shamelessness in their return,
a nauseating absurdity
in this repeated stealth of hope

Somewhere,
a year or two lay massacred
in the large vomit of time

And I am here,
again,

Against the cloud of Delhi dust;

just like one of those days I would travel from the hospital
and shiver along the barbecued roads,

Dwindling in the embrace of estrangement

Somewhere,
a year or two or three . . .
elapsed

But the air in my mouth
still feels like a sister,
sick and depleted—

just like it did when we first met

ON NIGHTMARES

Night breaks apart like pomegranate seeds in my palm.
The juice is everywhere, but can you really see things
when they spill?

There's only the smell and the incense of the heart
vomiting into the night.
The night has been cut short, the dream severed.

The dream, an octopus chewing the naked sense of being.
What strangeness that myth and reality come as twins?

As long as the juice burns the hand, its exotic smell slips
blood thawing on the wrist; it doesn't matter. I skip
paroxetine—

the aftertaste sings in my body like a Bloody Mary. In
the dream,
I am both dead and alive. I wake having swallowed
my very death.

In the dream, I am man, woman, animal and light—all
with a jarring sense of night. The night, a mad rider
with red hair.

In the dream, the mind eats the body and spits it to
make the day.
In the dream, I am the vivid strain of fear. I am bright
red and dimming

black. In the dream, I wish I were anything but this,
this ugliness, these damp sheets. This blindness,

how myth and reality come intertwined. Hard to say
which is which.

THE CONSTANT

The body listens
to its own beat,
the single reckless constant of life

I remember—once
it almost
slowed to a death song;

Its trepidations now beneath my tongue—
sewn tightly into suffocation

I depart in syllables,
roam as ash over china dolls

Clay models of life
hiding behind life-like fingers,
desperately reconstructing a semblance of hope

I roam—air
poisoned by its own composition

Grinding
through this strange machine of life,
this hiccupping device

It has no grace, no sense, no order
I must say
I'm rather displeased

It catches fire
but refuses to offer warmth
it wakes up—
a newborn baby
and wails,
wails against the fading night,
this night, that night, every other night

I watch the cold mist grow,
dandelions
over pale blue windows

Lung-like creatures—hanging, peeking,
moon-licked beauties
from winter's calculating mouth

I bite my fertile lip,
the stark taste of bile floods my eye
and I wonder

What are my chances at surviving this life?

DISENCHANTMENT

Hair withdraw
into the seamless blue night
and hang,

Hang behind the tilted neck,
the dome shoulders;

Their scraped minarets aglow
in the shadow cast
by the holy darkness of this splintered life

A joy emerges from the revolving tongue

Only the tongue,
only the tongue now knows
the distinct pleasure of separation,
of attachment and detachment

Spinning, arching,
tasting the desolate corridors
of days past and new,
days gone and days unforeseen

I have lived this
unnameable vastness of yours,
utterly still in my disenchantment

A frigid stasis—
a shadow, a lie,

the everlasting truth?

A stubborn silence seems to carry
these legs on a stretcher

A boat of beauty,
a theatre that only the precious few can attend—
death into life
and life shooting into death

THE LAST CELEBRATION

Death's swollen berry face
outside the window—
that always is
but isn't until it is

A clock
sucking on that beating squirrel heart,
a clock that continually ticks
until it hangs itself

A deluge of afternoons
red, red
vapours drown the curtain of life

You vanish into the sermon of days,
quietly ascending
the masochist note of the evening

Sit now—
legs crossed,
spread along the curvature of the night—
an entire black sea in the dot of your crinkled mouth

Stop
Stare
suspended there—in the triangle of life

the nose of darkness,
the shifting saliva of light

Between their wriggling gasps
of opium lovemaking—the periscope of life

Sit down—you
you, a stutter
you, who knows nothing,
but also too much

Sit
and slurp the last shiver;
watch the milk-white petals swim
along the scalp of an unfettered night

Night—her black velvet gown
finally dropping
between your besieged white eyes

II. Vertebrae-of-Thin-Light

THE-GARDEN-OF-DEATH

'Softly, it burns,
sonorous, bright,
cinnamon sticks splitting white fires,
the burning face of life'

These fingers—fishes and corpuscles,
deconstructed compartments

The hand—
a chase, a tale, a death, a dream, a fever
I am circles of continuous defeat,
defeat gathers defeat as dust gathers dust

Homes are constructed with uprooted flesh,
lives splattered—
spread beside wine on silver tables

Water,
I implore you to come,
point under point awaits—my cells evacuated

Skin rising in clots of red—
scattered red, found red, frothing red

Water, come, make this tract an ocean

Countless reflections
countless ripples

surgeries on the bone marrow
trickling days

Water,
come,
make death a garden
as I vacate

Everything occupies what was once not its—
space is inherited, taken, robbed

The only vacuum
is blood really
for it is filled with life—

life with its stomach slit
from the moment it makes its first contact with air

THE-WRIST-IS-A-RED-LOOP

Wrist by wrist
the blood sings
of its lives,
its many births
within the sands of death's naked breaths

I hear the cackling—
the blood has gone dry
red chalk, red rocks in teeth
dropping, falling
freefall

I am Christmas,
curtains and curtains of red,
sleek arms, raw, burnt umber

I watch,
my only spectator
I watch through wafer eyes—
the face, its wry horizon of pus cells

It comes to me like sex,
slow, gradual hymns
of nights rolling on widowed walls and windows

Windmills in the mouth
shredding every hint of knowledge

No language enters here
particles of air stand outside,
their red, potato faces swollen in shame

I know I'm a red song
that you once took in your arms,
mother

Once you sang to me
when the skies weren't poetry,
when the skies were just a faithful blue

Now they are scratched faces
of too many
days,
too many wailing days

Planets swim around my waist

HOW-MANY-DEATHS-MAKE-A-DREAM?

I walk,
clementine circles of the palm

The palm is a pond—
cold distilled blues, purple haze,
the cornea of a bearded mountain

Frog beside frog beside frog—
paddling feet occur in fumes,
an assembly of amphibian thoughts

I am—again
with my head of grains,
travelling across seas, inhaling ruins—
dead salt, dead flesh, dead breath

I am—again,
pondering—dwelling outside frigid lips
like a word on the way to a poem
What even remains of existence now but memory?

I am—again,
deducted and multiplied
picking my thoughts with a pair of tongs,
bangles of colors encircling nodes

Around my thumb,
a throat of black radish
emerges from slit flesh

And I am, again,
as I think
what is this dream . . .
what is this dream . . .

All with a promise of light under death

THE-BODY-IS-A-RED-EXOSKELETON

The body hangs above its organs,
a crime

Time is a crime
as I pin the epidermis to the wall,
ceiling's round face, candles cutting clouds

I am walking,
I am walking,
a ghost moon completing its rounds

Emerald-green water dragging its 24 feet
over bridges of faltering life

The ceiling drops
blood holds to itself in freefall
blood escaping blood, body escaping body

Fallen flesh,
blue eels above the fire extinguisher,
froth factories in breasts

Too many days have made the calendar blind
and now all anniversaries are of the dead

I carry the chewed edges of uneven days
and rub them on my tongue,
count the years—anticlockwise
in the second eye

Time is an altar
and my body hangs as a crime
organ burning organ, blood burning blood

THE-FIRST-FACE-IS-A-VALENTINE-RED

What is the reckoning for a stolen life?

The wrist cuts through the atmosphere—
twice in each circle,
reliving its own inexplicable birth

Each harvest the body must disintegrate,
petunias in a bald sky

Boxes of black skin
body into matter,
dead gums, dead fish, dead rain

I pick the remnants—membrane after membrane
roaming unabashedly on granite patches,
hopping on a single leg

A toothpick scratching
the perimeter of this maroon enclave,
square to square, mouth to mouth

Death came first
breaking the dam of that certain summer

The face streaming—
sunrise to sunset,
a nail on the white head

Containers of sacred blood,
mammal tongues
and cloaks of insidious love

What is it that love cannot hold, cannot take, cannot kill
once sworn? Love even swallows itself

It came,
came under
the quietness of open skin

A clock of dusty honeybees
slurping the roundness of my plump thigh,
its lather of brown nectar—
infestation, murder, love

THE-TONGUE-IS-A-PINK-CELLO

I.

Spread out like a tangential curve—
perched on window balconies,

I would stare at each abraded line of the sun.
the sky was my favourite thing, how if I lay

Horizontally, departed from the forces of
gravity and the will of life, everything was united.

A quiet murmur would rush across the diaphragm,
knots and levers humming slowly in joy

I was a djinn,
I didn't belong to this planet.

II.

In the hospital room, a pigeon perched
on the tooth of a transmission tower—

The flammable pink flakes on its neck
glistening at an unbearable pace.

Pigeons, I know them, they have been constant
companions—pecking in hostel rooms, getting pregnant

Right before my eyes, then laying insidious creatures
that slowly transformed into a yarn of mauve skin.

The sky here is a white ceiling;
a large, yellow light attempts to disembowel the mind.

I stare into its infinite brightness,
nothing returns.

III.

In my balcony, the leaves speak to each other,
I can feel their electrical voices as my fingers

Rush across their seamless lips.
the sky is now spread across the vertical face of the day,

Coagulated and starched as if announcing its infinite
dominion over us, over all earth.

In my balcony, a single sparrow—
the chirping so sweet it splits my skin.

A-LITTLE-HOPE-IS-A-RED-THING

I found hope on a soiled bed—
writhing beside me

She said that her body was a madhouse
that she had harboured too many
that she was guilty of unfathomable sins

I took the bedsheet
with its frenzied pattern of oranges
and levitating leaves

Slid my head into its bat-cave

Knots take knots with such endearment,
it's almost inhuman

I offered hope
the final lotus
from my spurting, red navel

Said it's all right,
my case of gleaming white teeth
a circus for the inner child

I said it's all right that you take one more
when you have taken so many;
my sisters are all now ready to fly

I draw carbon
with arms of spinning light,
the whiteness of night piercing my shell eye

Slivers of lost glaciers
course rapidly through my mouth
and as if by magic,
in a wink—
I disappear

A murmur of fatal nights

DILEMMA-OF-THE-RED-VALVES

What is that
between your toes?

That red pebble . . .
is it a condensed drop of rain

With the star swallowed in
its endless night?

Or is it . . .
a drop of blood? A tiny droplet

Taken from the place
your body sleeps, that deep chamber

Of dreams
What is it between your toes?

What do you hold, clutch
with such fierce love and blatant animosity?

What could receive the dual ends
of your being?

You carefully balance it,
each edge shining, glowing—

A newborn sun, a fatal sunset, a mad black
sky—all at the same time.

You carefully balance it
between ten thousand horizons and a million

Eternities. Your eyes—two gleaming pebbles,
so concrete, one would think

They belong to a dead God. What is that
you hold between your two toes?

That which you treasure and continually lose;

That where you grow
both restful and restless?

Is it; is it not your heart?

Your tiny heart between your toes
as if fallen from the heaven's arch.

Cytoplasm

A .

r .

d * o p let .

of b l o o d examines

it s e l

. f

. .

. . .

Drop by drop, blood almost kills itself; emerges again, both suicidal and invigorated. It searches for the wall, the boundary, the line, the curve of the jaw of life, the part where the teeth settle into a semblance of calm, of poise, the part where the tongue roams—pure flesh, pure desire, pure urge, pure suffering. Blood becomes foreign to itself, its many parts just hanging—limp, lipid, senseless and insane. Blood screams in the valley of the undiscovered, the unknown, the submerged. How can one possibly express that which cannot be ascertained, that which palpitates in the tongue and the throat and the vein and the leg, that which sings and pukes, that which is both nauseated and devoted, that which never dies but also never lives, that which rises forth along the centre of a blade of grass, that which exclaims absolute joy but also that which only knows how to scream? —And scream it does, until it isn't life and death duelling, but life against life against life.

| ___ | |

| :: | ___ | ::::::

| | ::::::

The city of dr 0 p...l:e:::ts

| | :: |

| ___

|

Droplets rise to the surface and fall flat upon their own skin. They are immersed now in the cataclysmic air, its groggy, violet hum. A stagnant body is perhaps the most violent. Its cheeks like tattered rafts against the long pause of day. It drifts in and out of material dreams, slips into the liver of slumber—a tirade of dark colourless endlessness. It is the sleep that knows only restlessness. I am here today as I was yesterday. I've been here before, too many times—I almost feel betrayed. I wish to twirl my fingers into tongs and drag the tongue out. Lick the silvery clot of thirsty red dust and say 'there'. 'There', 'there', anywhere but 'here'. Vowels breathe in the dark intestine of this being. This is where the bereft, the dead, the leftover skin is—the flimsy old warrior in her battle gown. It does not rest but flutter, flutter as an orphaned cloth under the torment of winter's steady breeze. It remains, restlessness in its sacred eyes, eyes of gold and green, eyes with rims of floating red, eyes that have seen, that have seen, that have seen.

. S

r e A

A red d op t E the s k y

. l T

.

Flesh drips over the palpitating mouth of time—the vascular gorge of amphibian fate. Condenses into patches. Burns. Conflagrates. Condenses. Patches and patches. Never has a forest seemed so worn, so dreary, so subtly misplaced.

The art of burning is lucid. It is the slick dance of sugar crackling over the arm of fire. The art of burning is intelligent. It is an algorithm that continuously revives itself, revises itself, reprimands itself. The art of burning is selfless. The art of burning is a mirror staring at a mirror staring at a mirror until the kaleidoscope is swallowed by the deluge of its own colours.

The syringe weaves the same song, over and over. It is rotating inside a hiccup. It spurts blood over the basin of time and only the face watches—aghast and empty, the solitary witness hollowed out by the misfortune of being. The syringe cuts into the fabric of senses and draws out a large trumpet—the hideous trumpet of death that is always whistling in the background, a widow dancing to the tune of lifelessness. The song of life clots into a ribbon and splits the sky into ten thousand halves, each demanding justice for itself. The blind, the wounded, the dishevelled, the massacred, the lesser, the unfortunate stand in a row and the sky blows up into a rhythm of dissonance—each shard demanding its share of divine love.

CACTUS

A surge/ a rift in the middle ground/ The barren sky of the eye shivers/ the eye that travels/ a seer in the darkness of time/ stiffening in the past/ in the present and all of arriving time/ A ray/ a thick red arrow/ convulses along the drag of the nose/ bloodied bowels of breath along the lip—the archangel in the holy sky of mouth/ Freckles around the chin/ the chin dropping into the cold hum of the precipitating air/ trickling slowly into the dreaming clavicle—the pool of sorrow/ the pool of collected joys/ Immersing into the tender outrage of blood/ The body of blood/ a black beast in the cleaved, starched sky/ the eagle flits through the fist and the fingers erupt into a most useless knowledge/ They travel through the currents of frothing air/ blood swirling in them/ steady/ slow/ now beaten/ now tired/ now very, very old in the grand passage of time/ Blood beats/ blood crawls/ blood screams in the panic of a still lake/ staring continuously outward/ vomiting in its own face/ The blood leaks and not a patch of ground/ not a stone/ not a chunk of ice/ not even the stray shadow from the window's edge takes notice/ Only the blood in its great fall/ swirling/ swirling/ continuously swirling in the cactus of time

ARTERY

I.

The peninsula of the feverish hand, the upturned hand, dwelling as a conundrum above strips of skinned air. Throbbing needlessly, desperately, throbbing in blue and lavender dots, a circus, a forest, an entire landscape of paleness. Winter's old confidante, grey and ancient, flowing steadily, rapidly, ravaging all in its path, coursing through the giant tributaries of blood vessels, their sputtering valleys, their saline consonance.

What is it that has been spoken? What have you learnt that you cannot forget? What is this disease that you have caught from the warm belly of the night that you cannot let go of? What is this desire that you conceal in your grand stutter? Why must you run in ambiguities, make of this fragile clockwork a carnival? What is it that holds your tongue and makes your limbs, your tiny feet run wild in me, day and night, night and night? What is this, what is this ugliness that you have sworn to be?

II.

In madness, reigns the eccentric song of the heart. The dreadful rose heart, almost terrified, almost smitten with its own severe palpitation. Its unquenchable need to be, its admirable desire to not. Suffering in its own arms, it gathers, it steals all the songs of the world from all the curious corners, the brightened edges, the bizarre waterfalls, the ever-wading roundness of things—a pervading haze. It is its own demise, rotting behind the schizophrenic eye of the mind, quivering behind thistles and needles. It is own demise and its own solitary reed, fluttering through the atmosphere, the blind sky, the all-pervading grey lake; hiding, then flinging itself in desperation into a bush of orange feathers, into the armpits of unknown birds, into raven eyes and abhorrent beauty, burning in innocence, the unendurable truth in its vascular scream.

III.

Spring forth, arms, from the remains of the day. Spread, seed by seed, knuckle by knuckle, eat the dust that glares from the edge. The wide-eyed sphere of air that watches with an unmistakable gaze, a hollow stare, the only one, the carcass of a large God, the aftermath of all truth and un-truth. Spring forth, arms, arms of restless ache, restless lisp, incurable restlessness, seek in the white fade of emptiness the echo of your being, your calamitous birth, your undying seed.

HIBISCUS

The blanket condenses in my soaked breath. My wet breath on its wide, cave-like structure, slipping through fingers, through the knots and gaps. Fever runs across the axis of the body. It glows; it blooms like a hibiscus—bright red. A hibiscus, I am, as I spread beneath the hovering air and count my days backwards. The days roll down my tongue as saliva, choking in parts, becoming in others. I am a large wound on this square-shaped bed. I lie with no imagination. My head—a bleached sack, my stomach—an army of pocketknives. Water bags erupt in the belly. There is that sound of war. Like all wars it is futile. Like all wars it is self-destructive. I feel the heat emerge, emerge and writhe in cuffs of air—vapours of skin and sweat-like flashes in the night sky. I am an incantation. I breathe and hiccup. I hiccup all over. Pain, they say, is a sensation in the mind. I have done it quite a few times, remembered this slogan. It almost works. Almost. And then it cracks open—a ball of plasma, hits every breathing thing in its wake. Pain, if you ask me, is the closest one comes to life, not death. For how can one deny its bubbling existence? It does not vanish with shut eyes. It cannot be removed by desperation. It traverses to the deepest cell and knocks. Pain is the closest one comes to reality. There are no illusions. There is only being and being and the endless mockery of it. In the stubbornness of the body, the great cry of the soul. The body leeched off by a thousand unnameable insects lies, glows in the dark with a red, hot fever, a band of molten iron and in the eyes—a glimmer, a glimmer of fleeting sense and hope.

DEBT

Turpentine sheen/ drooling droplets/ splattered/ veins of blue/ veins of yellow/ The holy trajectory of circles/ eddies washing their faces/ Monet's blue holding its tiny heartbeat in its own fist/ swish-swash/ flurry/ What is it that flies beneath? / Beneath and under/ under and above/ In the flimsy space where the water's large tongue sizzles/ dries into crisp waves and kills/ suspends as female heads and floats/ floats both dead and alive/ estranged and untied/ the song of a beautiful, moaning sea/ What is it that flies? / The river's body flopping/ surging through the slices of air/ travelling at the speed of blood/ What makes it possess this urgency? / This endless desire/ this/ this need/ this unspeakable event/ its course/ What is it that flows and flows and flows yet reaches nowhere? / Begins only once/ What is it that flows between two hands but never dies? / What is this? / This unspeakable word on the cliff of my throat/ this/ this which has been felt before/ I've known it/ this glorious madness of no end/ of only living/ this sickness of love that bursts through the two vertical halves of the body/ What is this but the ambition of life? / Bouncing between the same two moments/ birth and death/ never finding its answer/ Not in one body/ not in two/ a million lives and life still hiccups/ it flows and flows and flows/ always meeting death/ Never dying/ never beginning/ endlessness between two points/ What is this beauty that never ceases to be? / This madness of being/ this ceaseless offering of life to death/ this eternal debt/

PRAYER

The hammock of the night in its eternal sleep, oscillating and humming behind pursed lips. Occasionally, the tongue lunges forward and a prayer slips out, impalpable yet warm, minute yet pertinent. It is a fly causing trepidations in the extravagant suspension of time. Alongside the large heavy slumber of life, the tongue rolls downward and curls around the electric spasms of air, pollen drifting from stem to stem, bark to bark. Despite the encroaching dark and the tense mass of sickness, an echo precipitates, drools from the mouth. It is a word, a poem, a silence drawn from the veil. A prayer: restless, needy, bright, capable, full. A prayer, the first face of breath, the nude dance of dawn, the slur of a peacock's arms weaving into the turquoise stretch of rain. A prayer, the most foolish, the most, most foolish of all creatures lunges forward and begins to worship the tiniest of living things, the flowers, the bees, the ants—observing each stem and anther, each arch and echo as if they nested in their tiny girths all heavens and deities.

A GAP IN TIME

You watch a flower occur. Occur repeatedly, second after second, minute after minute. A flower is your pause. It holds your time while continuing its own, blooming, fuchsia blades flitting across the iris. A thread moves across simultaneous joys, weaving time, the abrasive touch of wind on its ductile skin. Details emerge as a creeping bush from the border of the eye. A flower gives you time by taking it away. Attention then is the most obvious response to beauty.

CRIB

Night squeezes into the fragrance of the living, the living in their ornate realms, adorned with garlands and beauty and breath. Night travels up the alley of flowers, plunging into their ripe tenderness, their careless joy, their unaware existence; the night that knows the sombre peace of non-existence and the contorted entropy of the verge. Night walks in, vast in its emptiness and kisses the flower, the mud, the dreaming tree, tasting their restlessness, the inherent buzz of their being; stretches its legs and purrs within the expanse of their hearts, the swarm of its copious absences finally meeting the sprouting fields of their aberrance.

HIDE-AND-SEEK

Mountains of light shift under breath: osmosis, exchange, and dance. The vertebra of space hesitates for existence. Bodies appear and reappear, vanish, and become in the cunning light. Bodies mould and collapse, morph, and shuffle. The cube changes with every thought, every movement, every word and lisp, an unpredictable, indecipherable dance. The chair changes its face too many times. It is a stranger at once. As is the wire, the lamp, the loose block of air.

I close my eyes.

Nothing happens except that the world is born again in my mouth—salivating, festering inside teeth as a loose argument, a parallel, dangling sightlessness. All sentences are felt but remain unseen. The orange fever of senselessness endures. Nothing enters but something escapes. Flesh upon flesh piles into a watery dream and slowly perspires into the night. I open my eyes and the world is a mute stranger. I close and I am one.

FLUTE

A tangent across the day/ a tooth/ a pointed tooth/ pressing against the creased loaf of lime skies/ A finger slips into the threadwork of dusk/ reaffirms its own existence/ A moment escapes/ and the tender pockets of clouds roam in the mouth/ rudiments and ash/ Nothing is quite as spectacular/ as beautiful/ as that which has ceased to exist/ that which roams neither in memory nor along the eye/ but traverses/ into the unknown/ the uncertain joy that sweetens the corners of the dreaming mouth/ An unnameable leaf/ twirling/ the continuous passage of daylight across bones/ across flesh/ across eyes/ A day conveniently forgotten/ carelessly strewn/ A day/ now nowhere to be found/ neither desired nor abandoned/ a day curling around the round ear/ The listless flute of being/

CURRANT

Look here. Look what sits—a single stone. A tiny stone in the middle of the white sands. I see its slimy contours—so black, so distinct as if continuously guarding something. Protecting from some ulterior reality. It has the night stored in its warm belly. The snail scratches on its skin appear as swollen nimbuses. I hold it in my palm and a muddied river meets the eye. A river now entrapped forever in its endless matter ring. Look, here, a tiny stone. Its smooth edges burn as if touching every eternity. I hold it in my palm and my veins flicker under the strange pressure—the stone's eternal secret. No one has unlocked it. It grows heavy, heavier. Like this body. Locking and choking, long, long dizziness. I take the stone and drop it into the sea. The sea eats the stone. The stone eats the sea.

ORIGAMI DREAM

I have a dream. I'm made of paper. A paper folding and unfolding, folding, unfolding. There is a scissor in my mouth and a cavity in my large stomach. I am a dream, a dream of paper. I'm almost done. I do not exist. I'm so thin I could compel myself into non-existence. Become the air that floats through me. I roam. I roam. I roam. I'm gay. I'm joy itself. I'm the tower of a building. I am a cable wire hanging in the eye of the sun. I am the shutter behind which the cat sleeps. I am its hallucination of pearl. I roam. I roam. I am the air itself. I own nothing and possess it all. I am the very wings of destiny. There is no destiny. There is time and time is in my mouth. It is a river between my teeth and my socks are birds prodding feed. I am the wing, the solitary wing that bursts through lovers' windows. I land on pigeon shit and I fly again into burgundy seas. I'm the very eye of the sun. I'm up, up and above. I sit atop the world. I'm a dream. I'm so light I do not exist. I'm so light that nothing could weigh me. I'm a dream, a paper dream, and nothing in the world ever reached a dream. I'm a dream, a paper dream; I'm alone and listless and free.

GONG—SONG OF LIFE

Shapes and songs floating, fluttering in the wild rage of open air. The songs of the air curled up like an insect in motion, alert and gleeful, joyous in the frenzy of a continuous flight, the hiccup of survival and fights. I count roses after roses as they traverse the trachea, tapping each bone and trinket, the slimy vessel of my being. A gong—my body, a gong—the tree, a gong—the shape-shifting shadow, a gong—the jaggery trail of soil, a gong—the rustling autumn dress, a gong—the affirmation in the sounds of leaves: sounds granting them life over and over, granting them breath in their prisons of stillness, in the celluloid cenotaphs of restlessness, in the trough of unquenchable spaces, the rings of losses, the vulnerability of nakedness—in patience, in the ceaseless patience of leaves against brevity; sparkling from twilight to eternity, in them gong—the air rustling through twig after twig after twig like a sea set to freedom in gravity.

INCENSE

An incense of breath flows between tall, white walls. A particle has settled on my cheek. I can feel its distilled blood. It flows into my veins and makes my arteries glow red. This, this incense of breath in the epileptic pollen dust eats my lips. Here I have sat, on the edge of things, calculating the intimacy between buildings and humans. Here I have sat, watched all life mimic each other in a glorious beat. Here, the child's swing hiccups against the corner of death, the pulse of life. I knock at the empty eyeball of air and find my body reverberating in the cold light. I knock and I am the singing tulip, its columns of light playing hide and seek. From the white hospital bed, the city has been swallowed by its own excretions. From the white hospital bed, everything can be seen in a single glance and beside me, a single tulip—its light shining in my wide mouth.

WOODPECKER

Something in the wind has beckoned a mourn. A small sliver of saliva leaps from the mouth, detaches from the tongue, and crawls. Why it rises one does not know . . . One cannot point to anything anymore, too many carcasses lie floating in the air. The air is suffused with pink so dense you'd think it would blind you. Pink, the colour of flesh—taut and thick, holding the seamlessness of red within. Pink, the first heaven. I open my chest; a woodpecker sits on it and scavenges in vain. It too perhaps searches for purpose in its actions, a life it does not comprehend, actions more swivelled by biology than choice. The woodpecker digs deep and finds nothing, only the mirror-like surface of my many deaths—a pallid fever, a surgeon's tools, naked blobs of pus, and the unbelievable endlessness of blood in life. The woodpecker, a tiny rose above my flat nipple, stares and digs, digs and stares. I, with my back against the grass, groan softly against the wet soil, spill in parts. I, with my back against the grass, spread unevenly. A clot of saliva now sits on the tip of my tongue, my tongue—a pale fortress in the air, a *kiss* and the tongue traverses, my mouth, my entire being in the woodpecker's endless swallow. The two of us on a flight: from up above—the glistening earth, our pale shadows submerged in the sky, *a small yelp*,
then the wide, aimless want of sorrow.

REVELATION

Lucid shapes run/ a dream's searing concoction/ a dream, half-awake/ a dream waking to its buttercup shadows/ its thick bristles/ its straying seams/ Lucid shapes move like tiny amoebae/ slowly at first and then large gulps of thought and memory/ The body eats air in surprises/ shuddering/ cold, velvet, and sweaty/ No arch forms in the sky/ only the cold, drenched day spreads into the soil/ Then collapses/ flat against the night and the two join for the first time/ Lips murmuring above the horizon/ meeting in glowing, viscous fluids/ Lucid shapes meet the eye/ claw the temporary skin of veils/ Trees hissing into large wounds/ tongues flaying every movement of every molecule/ the body sweating/ palpitating/ A cold, cold fever stretches into the very borders of darkness and then the red heavenly light of the fallen star/ The first star/ glows in the eye/ killing all mirages/ exploding reality/ turning light into dust/ Lucid shapes float/ the body hung between exposed truths/ awake in the current of illusionary life

NEELMOHAR IN A SULPHUR SKY

Neelmohar in a sulphur sky
                    stray spines, fervour of violet arms

Open is the sky's cleavage
stirring outside the window frame—
a yellow pigeon soup
with leeks and violet lights off uterine walls

Neelmohar,
your violet body moves along the meter of clouds

Air quaking/cubes and circles rolling/ shuffling/
pockets of winds
flocking between your ten thousand membrane-eyes

Neelmohar—you,
a giant squid morphing in the head of a yellow star

I open my palm
and I'm a dark violet raisin
I shadow myself—split endlessly through everything
I am neither the garden of death nor the burrow of life

Like you, I now wish to swim—bacteria, virus, fish,
amoeba, dinosaur—roll upon the wave that is blind

Neelmohar—
your giant arms squiggle in the daylight,
daylight—the face powder of sky,

glistening, matt bronze today, sparkling

Your movement is the undulating sea at night
cold scalp of an entire planet, layers and layers of thought,
a kind of omnipresence—

Like light when twig after twig clings to its precious life
and light—the non-entity, joyous and without, spills
from eye to lotus breast

There you are
neither life nor tree—neither particle nor wave
but a blurring phase between the two

A sweet pocket of *jamuns* in my mouth—juice sliding into gut
and ice

There you are—the frenzied shape of movement
            a clip in time is just air
motionless motion,
the medium in which dust glows brightest—you and I

Neelmohar—your hair, upturned braids teasing the air

The yellow sky drains
as the pus that's been hiding inside the ear;
you never know where it's risen. You only know it—
the borders of life akin to smells—pungent, invisible

You dance in the yellow stone—endlessness
a particle stirring, stirring above the surface tension
of all life, floating—its mouth agape

There is no accuracy that can hold this emotion
language must slide away too—as life enters

Neelmohar—
your bright, bright purple being like a flood in the mouth,
the whale sea that squat in the body's velveteen form,
cocooned and then awake—

Rushing, rushing, tenderly claiming that all is it, all is it

There it is—you—earth's feverish sleep that none touched
there it is—the clot of blood that floated into the skull—
never to be found again, now a gargantuan sea—a breath of its own
cells and cells and cells

There it is, Neelmohar—
your sharp movements in space dulled by the thread of the eye
waves, lines, lines—stacked into an ocean
the body collapsed into a fever—

Light like a rod across all being

FRINGE

On the leaf,
sediments of dispersed days

In the floating shadow,
a recollection of being

Hovering above,
amidst strands of resin air,
a cut in time, a bumblebee strumming distance

Across the wind,
a leaping anxiety
wafting bubbles in my mouth

Above the eyelid, restlessness—
beneath which the blue iris sinks,
tethered tides in its osmotic sea

I stretch into the unimaginable,
the inconceivable,
the suspended lotus

I stretch into the
white circle,
my waist, a drawn-out sea

There is no rhythm to levitation, only energy

It takes a flower to bloom
and a flower to learn

how one must wilt—
to offer beauty even in death